G000152176

YOU MAKE ME PROUD

summersdale

YOU MAKE ME PROUD

This edition copyright © Summersdale Publishers Ltd, 2020

First published in 2017

An Hachette UK Company
www.hachette.co.uk

Summersdale Publishers Ltd
Part of Octopus Publishing Group Limited
Carmelite House
50 Victoria Embankment
LONDON
EC4Y 0DZ
UK

www.summersdale.com

Printed and bound in China

ISBN: 978-1-78783-552-8

Substantial discounts on bulk quantities of Summersdale books are available to corporations, professional associations and other organizations. For details contact general enquiries: telephone: +44 (0) 1243 771107 or email: enquiries@summersdale.com.

TO.............................

FROM.........................

To be yourself in a world that is constantly trying to make you something else is the greatest accomplishment.

RALPH WALDO EMERSON

Mastering others
is strength.
Mastering yourself
is true power.

LAO TZU

YOU'VE COME SO
FAR FROM WHERE
YOU STARTED

With ordinary talent and extraordinary perseverance, all things are attainable.

THOMAS FOWELL BUXTON

Difficulties are things that show a person what they are.

EPICTETUS

We don't even know how strong we are until we are forced to bring that hidden strength forward.

ISABEL ALLENDE

YOU
DESERVE
EVERY
SUCCESS

Believe you can and you're halfway there.

THEODORE ROOSEVELT

The roughest
roads often lead
to the top.

CHRISTINA AGUILERA

YOU
ARE SO
STRONG

The world you
desire can be won.
It exists... it is real...
it is possible...
it's yours.

AYN RAND

Those who
wish to sing always
find a song.

SWEDISH PROVERB

Optimism is essential to achievement and it is also the foundation of courage.

NICHOLAS MURRAY BUTLER

DON'T TELL
PEOPLE
YOUR DREAMS.
SHOW THEM.

You can't stop the waves, but you can learn to surf.

JON KABAT-ZINN

You may never
know what results
come from your
actions, but if you
do nothing, there
will be no results.

MAHATMA GANDHI

YOU

ARE

AMAZING!

The more we
do, the more
we can do.

WILLIAM HAZLITT

To accomplish great things,
we must not only act,
but also dream; not only
plan but also believe.

ANATOLE FRANCE

What we see depends mainly on what we look for.

JOHN LUBBOCK

YOU ARE
THE CREATOR OF
YOUR FUTURE

**Don't let what
you cannot do
interfere with what
you can do.**

JOHN R. WOODEN

Success is the sum of small efforts, repeated day in and day out.

ROBERT COLLIER

THERE'S NOTHING YOU CAN'T DO

Act as if what
you do makes a
difference. It does.

WILLIAM JAMES

Plunge boldly into the thick of life, and seize it where you will, it is always interesting.

JOHANN WOLFGANG VON GOETHE

You gain strength, courage and confidence by every experience in which you really stop to look fear in the face.

ELEANOR ROOSEVELT

YOUR LIFE IS
AS GOOD AS
YOUR MINDSET

**Never give in –
never, never,
never, never.**

WINSTON CHURCHILL

Every man is the architect of his own fortune.

APPIUS CLAUDIUS CAECUS

HAVE FAITH
IN YOURSELF

Just when the caterpillar thought the world was over, it became a butterfly.

ANONYMOUS

You are never too old to set a new goal or dream a new dream.

LES BROWN

Success is only meaningful and enjoyable if it feels like your own.

MICHELLE OBAMA

BE PROUD OF
WHO YOU ARE
AND ALL YOU'VE
OVERCOME

Perseverance is stubbornness with a purpose.

JOSH SHIPP

It's kind of fun to
do the impossible.

WALT DISNEY

WHEREVER YOU GO, GO WITH ALL YOUR HEART

The difference between perseverance and obstinacy is that one comes from a strong will and the other from a strong won't.

HENRY WARD BEECHER

Be yourself.
The world worships
the original.

INGRID BERGMAN

When patterns are broken, new worlds emerge.

TULI KUPFERBERG

BELIEVE IN HOW FAR YOU CAN GO

The secret of getting ahead is getting started.

MARK TWAIN

Things work out best for those who make the best of the way things work out.

ANONYMOUS

IF IT DOESN'T OPEN, IT'S NOT YOUR DOOR

Don't let them
tame you.

ISADORA DUNCAN

Just be yourself,
there is no one
better.

TAYLOR SWIFT

There is only one map to the journey of life and it lives within your heart.

WILLIE NELSON

IT TAKES COURAGE TO BE YOURSELF

It's easy to make a buck. It's a lot tougher to make a difference.

TOM BROKAW

YOU ARE
SIGNIFICANT

If you're going to
doubt something, doubt
your own limits.

DON WARD

**Trust yourself.
You know more than
you think you do.**

BENJAMIN SPOCK

Every strike brings me closer to the next home run.

BABE RUTH

One may walk
over the highest
mountain one
step at a time.

JOHN WANAMAKER

PROVE THEM WRONG!

I'm convinced that about
half of what separates
successful entrepreneurs
from the non-successful
ones is pure perseverance.

———————

STEVE JOBS

Dare to love
yourself as if you
were a rainbow with
gold at both ends.

ABERJHANI

TAKE PRIDE
IN HOW FAR
YOU'VE COME

Champions keep playing until they get it right.

BILLIE JEAN KING

**Turn your face
toward the sun and
the shadows will
fall behind you.**

MĀORI PROVERB

**Don't go through
life; grow through life.**

ERIC BUTTERWORTH

KEEP GOING

No one can do everything, but everyone can do something.

MAX LUCADO

The potential
for greatness lives
within each of us.

WILMA RUDOLPH

DO WHAT YOU THINK YOU CANNOT DO

I am a slow walker, but I never walk back.

ABRAHAM LINCOLN

The will to persevere is often the difference between failure and success.

DAVID SARNOFF

Nothing is impossible.
The word itself says
"I'm possible"!

AUDREY HEPBURN

YOUR ONLY LIMIT IS YOUR MIND

Obstacles are the
raw materials of great
accomplishment.

TOMMY NEWBERRY

A strong, positive self-image is the best possible preparation for success.

JOYCE BROTHERS

YOU DESERVE TO BE PROUD OF YOURSELF

The best way
out is always
through.

ROBERT FROST

It's always
too early to quit.

NORMAN VINCENT PEALE

Perseverance is not a long race; it is many short races one after the other.

WALTER ELLIOT

WHAT YOU
DO MAKES A
DIFFERENCE

Run your own
race of life, with
a single-minded
vision of purpose.

LAILAH GIFTY AKITA

Who seeks
shall find.

SOPHOCLES

BELIEVE
YOU CAN AND
YOU WILL

The worst enemy
to creativity is
self-doubt.

SYLVIA PLATH

When everything seems
to be going against you,
remember that the airplane
takes off against the wind.

HENRY FORD

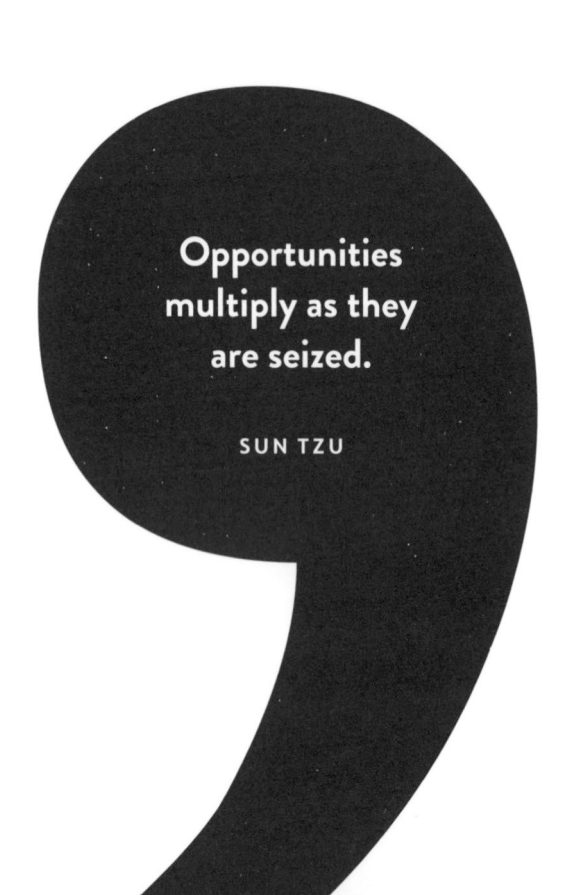

Opportunities multiply as they are seized.

SUN TZU

OWN WHO

YOU

ARE

What lies
behind you and
what lies in front
of you, pales in
comparison to what
lies inside of you.

RALPH WALDO EMERSON

You don't get
harmony when everyone
sings the same note.

DOUG FLOYD

DIRECTION
IS MORE
IMPORTANT
THAN SPEED

For myself I am an optimist – it does not seem to be much use to be anything else.

WINSTON CHURCHILL

One person can
make a difference,
and everyone should try.

JOHN F. KENNEDY

Dare to be different
and to set your own
pattern, live your
own life and follow
your own star.

WILFERD PETERSON

TURN YOUR DREAMS INTO PLANS

If you can imagine it, you can achieve it. If you can dream it, you can become it.

WILLIAM ARTHUR WARD

Your time is limited, so don't waste it living someone else's life.

STEVE JOBS

GET THERE

YOU WILL

It does not matter how
slowly you go as long
as you do not stop.

CONFUCIUS

First, think.
Second, believe.
Third, dream.
And finally, dare.

WALT DISNEY

Don't count the days, make the days count.

MUHAMMAD ALI

YOU HAVE
EVERYTHING
YOU NEED

Your soul is all that you possess. Take it in hand and make something of it!

MARTIN H. FISCHER

In the middle
of difficulty lies
opportunity.

ALBERT EINSTEIN

TRUST
YOURSELF

Achievement is not always success... It is honest endeavour, persistent effort to do the best possible under any and all circumstances.

ORISON SWETT MARDEN

Don't give up.
Don't lose hope.
Don't sell out.

CHRISTOPHER REEVE

**No one succeeds
without effort...
Those who succeed
owe their success
to perseverance.**

RAMANA MAHARSHI

NOTHING WORTH HAVING COMES EASY

If you fell down yesterday, stand up today.

H. G. WELLS

We have to dare to
be ourselves, however
frightening or strange
that self may prove to be.

MAY SARTON

STARS
CAN'T
SHINE
WITHOUT
DARKNESS

We may encounter
many defeats but we
must not be defeated.

MAYA ANGELOU

If opportunity doesn't knock, build a door.

MILTON BERLE

Anything you really want, you can attain, if you really go after it.

WAYNE DYER

POSITIVITY IS COURAGEOUS

These are the days
that must happen to you.

WALT WHITMAN

It all begins and ends in your mind. What you give power to has power over you, if you allow it.

LEON BROWN

THIS DAY
IS YOURS

If you celebrate
your differentness,
the world will, too.

VICTORIA MORAN

Just throw away
all thoughts of
imaginary things,
and stand firm in
that which you are.

KABIR

What progress, you ask, have I made? I have begun to be a friend to myself.

HECATO

YOU HAVE
THE POWER
TO CREATE
CHANGE

You are perfectly cast in your life. I can't imagine anyone but you in the role. Go play.

LIN-MANUEL MIRANDA

What I am is good
enough if I would
only be it openly.

CARL ROGERS

Only in the darkness can you see the stars.

MARTIN LUTHER KING JR

HAVE THE
COURAGE
OF YOUR
CONVICTIONS

The best way to predict the future is to invent it.

ALAN KAY

What would life be if
we had no courage to
attempt anything?

VINCENT van GOGH

IT'S NEVER
TOO LATE

Remember, if you ever
need a helping hand, it's
at the end of your arm.

SAM LEVENSON

**Follow your
honest convictions,
and stay strong.**

WILLIAM MAKEPEACE THACKERAY

GIVE UP

NEVER

Everything you've ever wanted is on the other side of fear.

GEORGE ADDAIR

There is just one
life for each of
us: our own.

EURIPIDES

The final forming of a
person's character lies
in their own hands.

ANNE FRANK

STAY
STRONG

The harder the conflict, the more glorious the triumph.

THOMAS PAINE

You have to
be unique, and
different, and shine
in your own way.

LADY GAGA

WHEN YOU CAN'T SING, HUM

Life is a pure flame, and we live by an invisible sun within us.

THOMAS BROWNE

Do what you can,
with what you have,
where you are.

THEODORE ROOSEVELT

There is no magic to achievement. It's really about hard work, choices and persistence.

MICHELLE OBAMA

YOU CAN DO IT; ALL YOU HAVE TO DO IS TRY

It takes courage
to grow up and
become who you
really are.

E. E. CUMMINGS

**Your attitude,
not your aptitude,
will determine
your altitude.**

ZIG ZIGLAR

KEEP

YOUR

HEAD UP

What we do flows from who we are.

CHARLES COLSON

Every day brings a chance
for you to draw in a breath,
kick off your shoes, and dance.

OPRAH WINFREY

What's meant
to be will always
find a way.

TRISHA YEARWOOD

YOU ARE CAPABLE

OF AMAZING

THINGS

Fortune favours the bold.

LATIN PROVERB

Do your little bit of good where you are; it's those little bits of good put together that overwhelm the world.

DESMOND TUTU

Respect yourself
and others will
respect you.

CONFUCIUS

YOU ARE IN CONTROL OF YOUR OWN LIFE

Accept no one's definition
of your life; define yourself.

HARVEY FIERSTEIN

Follow your own star.

DANTE ALIGHIERI

When you're
true to who you
are, amazing
things happen.

DEBORAH NORVILLE

Make the most of yourself
by fanning the tiny, inner
sparks of possibility into
flames of achievement.

GOLDA MEIR